This edition published 1994 by Dean,
in association with Heinemann Young Books
an imprint of Reed Children's Books
Michelin House, 81 Fulham Road, London SW3 6RB
and Auckland, Melbourne, Singapore and Toronto
This presentation copyright © 1994 William Heinemann Ltd
Text devised by Alison Green copyright
© 1994 Reed International Books Limited
Illustrations by Ken Stott copyright
© 1991, 1993, 1994 Reed International Books Limited

Printed in Great Britain

ISBN 0 603 55367 2

A CIP catalogue record for this book is available from the British Library.

Thomas the Tank Engine's European Word Book

ENGLISH **FRENCH** *GERMAN*

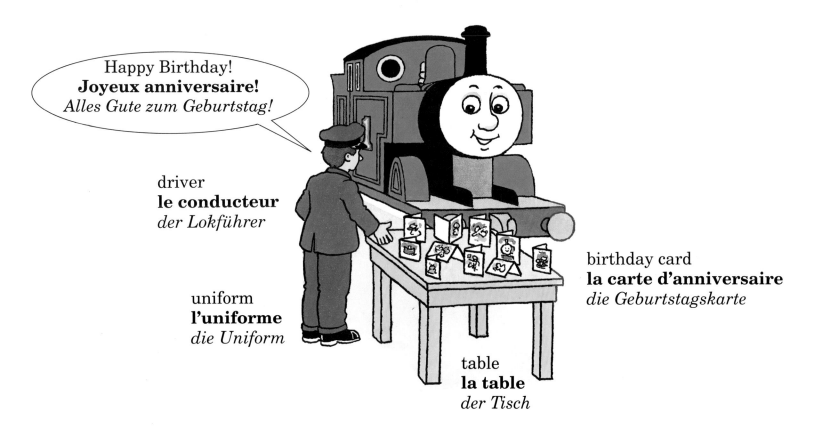

Happy Birthday!
Joyeux anniversaire!
Alles Gute zum Geburtstag!

driver
le conducteur
der Lokführer

uniform
l'uniforme
die Uniform

birthday card
la carte d'anniversaire
die Geburtstagskarte

table
la table
der Tisch

Christopher Awdry • Ken Stott

DEAN

Contents

Engines
Les Locomotives
Die Lokomotiven

Edward

Duck

James

Toby

Gordon

Donald

We're twins.
Nous sommes jumeaux.
Wir sind Zwillinge.

I am a really useful engine.
Je suis une locomotive vraiment utile.
Ich bin eine sehr nützliche Lokomotive.

Douglas

Thomas

I'm little.
Je suis petit.
Ich bin klein.

I'm cheerful.
Je suis joyeux.
Ich bin fröhlich.

Percy

Henry

Which is your favourite engine?
Quelle est ta locomotive préférée?
Welche Lokomotive hast du am liebsten?

9

At the Seaside
Au Bord de la Mer
Am Meer

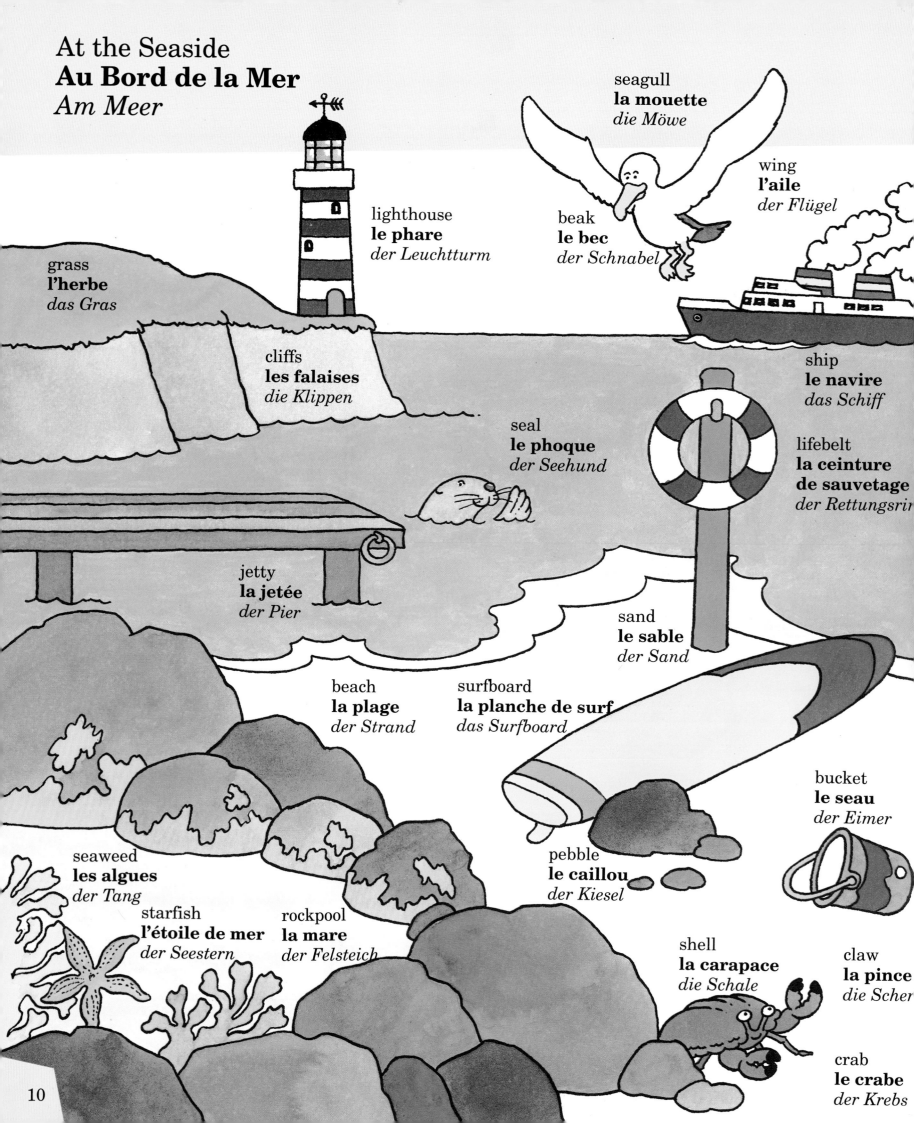

seagull
la mouette
die Möwe

wing
l'aile
der Flügel

beak
le bec
der Schnabel

lighthouse
le phare
der Leuchtturm

grass
l'herbe
das Gras

cliffs
les falaises
die Klippen

ship
le navire
das Schiff

seal
le phoque
der Seehund

lifebelt
**la ceinture
de sauvetage**
der Rettungsrin

jetty
la jetée
der Pier

sand
le sable
der Sand

beach
la plage
der Strand

surfboard
la planche de surf
das Surfboard

bucket
le seau
der Eimer

seaweed
les algues
der Tang

pebble
le caillou
der Kiesel

starfish
l'étoile de mer
der Seestern

rockpool
la mare
der Felsteich

shell
la carapace
die Schale

claw
la pince
die Scher

crab
le crabe
der Krebs

Ben and Polly are playing on the beach.
Ben et Polly jouent sur la plage.
Ben und Polly spielen am Strand.

sky
le ciel
der Himmel

Harold the helicopter
Harold l'hélicoptère
Harold der Hubschrauber

flag
le drapeau
die Flagge

horizon
l'horizon
der Horizont

mast
le mât
der Mast

sail
la voile
das Segel

buoy
la bouée
die Boje

rock
le rocher
der Stein

sailing boat
le voilier
das Segelboot

sea
la mer
das Meer

seashore
le bord de la mer
der Strand

wave
la vague
die Welle

thermos flask
le thermos
die Thermosflasche

girl
la fille
das Mädchen

rubber ring
**la bouée
en caoutchouc**
der Schwimmring

boy **le garçon**
der Junge

swimsuit
le maillot
der Badeanzug

bag
le sac
die Tasche

spade
la pelle
die Schaufel

sandcastle
le château de sable
die Sandburg

towel
la serviette
das Handtuch

ball
le ballon
der Ball

11

The Body
Le Corps
Der Körper

head
la tête
der Kopf

neck
le cou
der Hals

shoulder
l'épaule
die Schulter

chest
la poitrine
die Brust

arm
le bras
der Arm

stomach
le ventre
der Bauch

wrist
le poignet
das Handgelenk

thigh
la cuisse
der Oberschenkel

ankle
la cheville
der Knöchel

foot
le pied
der Fuß

My nails are called claws.
Mes ongles s'appellent des griffes.
Meine Nägel nennt man Krallen.

whiskers
les moustaches
die Schnurrhaare

tail
la queue
der Schwanz

claw
la griffe
die Klaue

hair
les cheveux
das Haar

cheek
la joue
die Backe

elbow
le coude
der Ellbogen

thumb
le pouce
der Daumen

ear
l'oreille
das Ohr

back
le dos
der Rücken

hand
la main
die Hand

fur
le poil
das Fell

muzzle
le museau
das Maul

bottom
le derrière
der Po

finger
le doigt
der Finger

paw
la patte
die Pfote

leg
la jambe
das Bein

toe
l'orteil
die Zehe

knee
le genou
das Knie

My foot is called a paw.
Mon pied s'appelle une patte.
Meinen Fuß nennt man eine Pfote.

12

The Engine
La Locomotive
Die Lokomotive

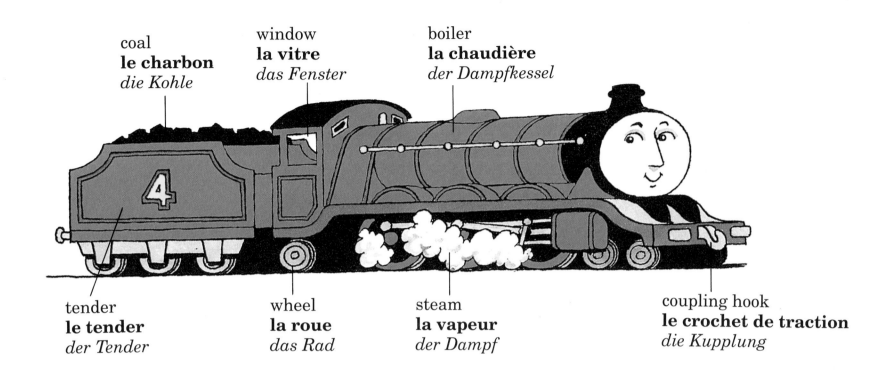

coal
le charbon
die Kohle

window
la vitre
das Fenster

boiler
la chaudière
der Dampfkessel

tender
le tender
der Tender

wheel
la roue
das Rad

steam
la vapeur
der Dampf

coupling hook
le crochet de traction
die Kupplung

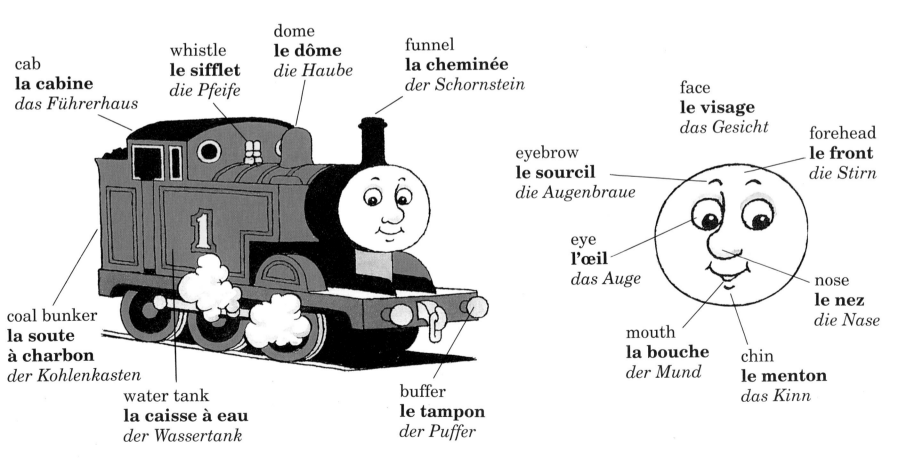

cab
la cabine
das Führerhaus

whistle
le sifflet
die Pfeife

dome
le dôme
die Haube

funnel
la cheminée
der Schornstein

face
le visage
das Gesicht

forehead
le front
die Stirn

eyebrow
le sourcil
die Augenbraue

eye
l'œil
das Auge

nose
le nez
die Nase

coal bunker
**la soute
à charbon**
der Kohlenkasten

water tank
la caisse à eau
der Wassertank

buffer
le tampon
der Puffer

mouth
la bouche
der Mund

chin
le menton
das Kinn

Clothes
Les Vêtements
Die Kleidung

Which are your favourite clothes?
Quels sont tes vêtements préférés?
Welche Kleider hast du am liebsten?

mirror
le miroir
der Spiegel

sleeve
la manche
der Ärmel

button
le bouton
der Knopf

waistcoat
le gilet
die Weste

man
l'homme
der Mann

woman
la femme
die Frau

cap
la casquette
die Mütze

tie
la cravate
der Schlips

jacket
la veste
die Jacke

necklace
le collier
die Halskette

uniform
l'uniforme
die Uniform

belt
la ceinture
der Gürtel

suit
le costume
der Anzug

cuff
la manchette
die Manschette

trousers
le pantalon
die Hose

dress
la robe
das Kleid

guard
le chef de train
der Schaffner

briefcase
la serviette
die Aktentasche

shoe
la chaussure
der Schuh

hat
le chapeau
der Hut

scarf
l'écharpe
das Halstuch

glove
le gant
der Handschuh

coat
le manteau
der Mantel

handbag
le sac à main
die Handtasche

mitten
la moufle
der Fäustling

skirt
la jupe
der Rock

boot
la botte
der Stiefel

umbrella
le parapluie
der Regenschirm

duffelcoat
le duffel-coat
der Dufflecoat

tights
le collant
die Strumpfhose

collar
le col
der Kragen

cardigan
le cardigan
die Strickjacke

blouse
la blouse
die Bluse

pocket
la poche
die Tasche

jeans
le jean
die Jeans

shirt
la chemise
das Oberhemd

dungarees
la salopette
die Latzhosen

jumper
le pullover
der Pullover

t-shirt
le tee-shirt
das T-Shirt

plimsoll
la basquette
der Turnschuh

shorts
le short
die Shorts

goal
le but
das Tor

sock
la chaussette
der Kniestrumpf

football boots
les bottes de football
die Fußballschuhe

tap
le robinet
der Hahn

lamp
la lampe
die Lampe

pillow
l'oreiller
das Kopfkissen

dressing gown
la robe de chambre
der Morgenrock

blanket
la couverture
die Decke

toothbrush
**la brosse
à dents**
die Zahnbürste

towel
la serviette
das Handtuch

toothpaste
le dentifrice
die Zahncreme

washbasin
le lavabo
das Waschbecken

bed
le lit
das Bett

sheet
le drap
das Bettuch

nightdress
la chemise de nuit
das Nachthemd

slipper
la pantoufle
der Pantoffel

pyjamas
le pyjama
der Schlafanzug

bedside table
la table de nuit
der Nachttisch

teddy bear
le nounours
der Teddybär

15

poster
l'affiche
das Plakat

lamp
la lampe
die Laterne

flag
le drapeau
die Flagge

whistle
le sifflet
die Pfeife

buffers
les tampons
der Prellbock

bench
le banc
die Bank

guard
le chef de train
der Schaffner

mail-bag
le sac postal
der Postsack

crate
la caisse
die Kiste

Where are my bucket and spade?
Où sont ma pelle et mon seau?
Wo sind mein Eimer und meine Schaufel?

16

Gordon the big engine
Gordon la grande locomotive
Gordon die große Lokomotive

dome
le dôme
die Haube

TICKET OFFICE

clock
l'horloge
die Uhr

steam
la vapeur
der Dampf

platform
le quai
der Bahnsteig

ticket office
le guichet
der Fahrkartenschalter

suitcase
la valise
der Koffer

MAIL

trolley
le chariot
der Gepäckwagen

porter
le porteur
der Gepäckträger

trunk
la malle
der Schrankkoffer

Ben and Polly have lost their bucket and spade at the station.
Ben et Polly ont perdu leur pelle et leur seau à la gare.
*Ben und Polly haben ihren Eimer und ihre Schaufel
am Bahnhof verloren.*

hat-box
le carton à chapeau
die Hutschachtel

17

Shapes
Les Formes
Die Formen

What shape is the window?
De quelle forme est la fenêtre?
Welche Form hat das Fenster?

What shape is my face?
De quelle forme est mon visage?
Welche Form hat mein Gesicht?

windowpane
la vitre
die Fensterscheibe

window
la fenêtre
das Fenster

corner
l'angle
die Ecke

Can you see my bell?
Vois-tu ma cloche?
Kannst du meine Glocke sehen?

sky
le ciel
der Himmel

star
l'étoile
der Stern

I can see stars.
Je vois des étoiles.
Ich sehe die Sterne.

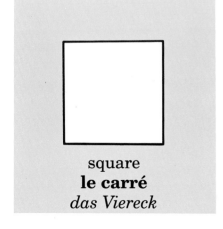

square
le carré
das Viereck

circle
le rond
der Kreis

bell
la cloche
die Glocke

star
l'étoile
der Stern

What shape is the picture?
De quelle forme est le tableau?
Welche Form hat das Bild?

portrait
le portrait
das Porträt

frame
le cadre
der Rahmen

earth
la terre
die Erde

flowerbed
la plate-bande
das Blumenbeet

trowel
le déplantoir
die Kelle

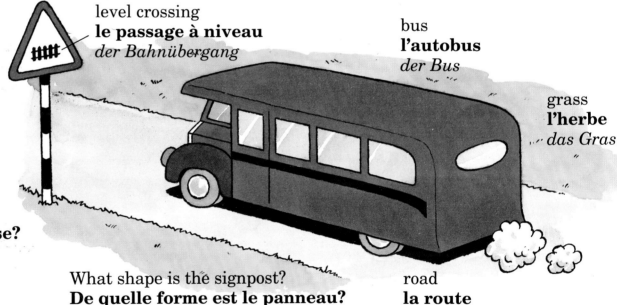

What shape is the flowerbed?
De quelle forme est la plate-bande?
Welche Form hat das Blumenbeet?

signpost
le panneau de signalisation
das Verkehrszeichen

handle
la poignée
der Henkel

suitcase
la valise
der Koffer

level crossing
le passage à niveau
der Bahnübergang

bus
l'autobus
der Bus

grass
l'herbe
das Gras

What shape is the suitcase?
De quelle forme est la valise?
Welche Form hat der Koffer?

What shape is the signpost?
De quelle forme est le panneau?
Welche Form hat das Verkehrszeichen?

road
la route
die Straße

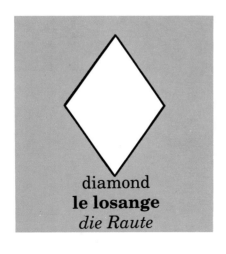

oval
l'ovale
das Oval

diamond
le losange
die Raute

rectangle
le rectangle
das Rechteck

triangle
le triangle
das Dreieck

The Days of the Week
Les Jours de la Semaine
Die Tage der Woche

I'm going to school.
Je vais à l'école.
Ich gehe in die Schule.

Monday
lundi
Montag

What day is it today?
Quel jour sommes-nous aujourd'hui?
Welcher Tag ist heute?

I'm going to work.
Je vais au travail.
Ich gehe zur Arbeit.

Tuesday
mardi
Dienstag

Thursday
jeudi
Donnerstag

Wednesday
mercredi
Mittwoch

I'm watching the parade.
Je regarde la parade.
Ich sehe der Parade zu.

I'm going riding.
Je vais monter à cheval.
Ich gehe reiten.

Friday
vendredi
Freitag

I'm going shopping.
Je vais faire des courses.
Ich gehe einkaufen.

We're going to the beach.
Nous allons à la plage.
Wir gehen an den Strand.

Saturday and Sunday
samedi et dimanche
Samstag und Sonntag

Special Days
Les Jours de Fête
Feiertage

Happy Birthday!
Joyeux anniversaire!
Alles Gute zum Geburtstag!

Happy New Year!
Bonne année!
Frohes neues Jahr!

balloon
le ballon
der Luftballon

Cheers!
A votre santé!
Prost!

New Year's Day
le Jour de l'An
der Neujahrstag

sandwich
le sandwich
die Schnitte

Happy Easter!
Joyeuses Pâques!
Frohe Ostern!

candle
la bougie
die Kerze

birthday card
la carte d'anniversaire
die Geburtstagskarte

birthday cake
le gâteau d'anniversaire
der Geburtstagskuchen

birthday
l'anniversaire
der Geburtstag

Easter eggs
les œufs de Pâques
die Ostereier

Easter Day
Pâques
Ostersonntag

star
l'étoile
der Stern

Christmas tree
le sapin de Noël
der Weihnachtsbaum

daffodil
la jonquille
die Narzisse

bouquet of flowers
le bouquet de fleurs
der Blumenstrauß

Christmas Day
le jour de Noël
der erste Weihnachtstag

present
le cadeau
das Geschenk

tulip
la tulipe
die Tulpe

Happy Christmas everyone!
Joyeux Noël à tout le monde!
Fröhliche Weihnachten allerseits!

Mothers' Day
la Fête des Mères
der Muttertag

Father Christmas
le père Noël
der Weihnachtsmann

21

In the Ticket Office
Au Guichet
Am Fahrkartenschalter

clock
l'horloge
die Uhr

timetable
l'horaire
der Fahrplan

TIMETABLE	
AM.	P.M.
6·00	1·00
6·30	2·15
7·00	3·00
7·30	4·00
9·00	4·30
9·30	5·00
10·00	7·00
11·30	9·00

file
le classeur
der Aktenordner

ticket **le billet**
die Fahrkarte

traveller
le voyageur
der Reisende

PRICES
SINGLE - £5·00
RETURN - £10·00
CHILD £2·50
DOG £1·00
CAT £0·50

price list
la liste des prix
die Preisliste

season ticket
**la carte
d'abonnement**
die Zeitkarte

ticket clerk
le marchand de billets
der Fahrkartenverkäufer

briefcase
la serviette
die Aktentasche

cupboard
le placard
der Schrank

drawer
le tiroir
die Schublade

stool
le tabouret
der Hocker

floor
le sol
der Fußboden

money
l'argent
das Geld

fountain pen
le stylo à encre
der Füller

key
la clef
der Schlüssel

chair
la chaise
der Stuhl

cashbox
la caisse
die Geldkassette

Ben and Polly's bucket and spade aren't in the ticket office.
La pelle et le seau de Ben et Polly ne se trouvent pas au guichet.
Der Eimer und die Schaufel von Ben und Polly sind nicht beim Fahrkartenschalter.

calendar
le calendrier
der Kalender

wall
le mur
die Wand

jacket
la veste
die Jacke

I'm sorry.
Je suis désolé.
Es tut mir leid.

manager
le directeur
der Geschäftsführer

door
la porte
die Tür

safe
le coffre-fort
der Safe

station cat
le chat de la gare
die Bahnhofskatze

rug   **le tapis**   *der Teppich*

23

The Weather
Le Temps
Das Wetter

What's the weather like today?
Quel temps fait-il aujourd'hui?
Wie ist das Wetter heute?

My hat!
Mon chapeau!
Mein Hut!

wind
le vent
der Wind

rainbow
l'arc-en-ciel
der Regenbogen

It's freezing.
Il gèle.
Es friert.

ice
la glace
das Eis

Help!
Au secours!
Hilfe!

roots
les racines
die Wurzeln

snow
la neige
der Schnee

I'm stuck!
Je suis bloqué!
Ich komme nicht weiter!

snowdrift
la congère
die Schneewehe

hurricane
l'ouragan
der Orkan

lightning
l'éclair
der Blitz

sun
le soleil
die Sonne

sunglasses
les lunettes de soleil
die Sonnenbrille

I'm scared.
J'ai peur.
Ich habe Angst.

It's hot.
Il fait chaud.
Es ist heiß.

thunder
le tonnerre
der Donner

storm
l'orage
der Sturm

I'm hiding.
Je me cache.
Ich verstecke mich.

cloud
le nuage
die Wolke

Where is he?
Où est-il?
Wo ist er?

I'm not coming out!
Je ne vais pas sortir!
Ich gehe nicht hinaus!

I can't see!
Je n'y vois rien!
Ich kann nichts sehen!

rain
la pluie
der Regen

fog
le brouillard
der Nebel

raindrop
la goutte de pluie
der Regentropfen

Opposites
Les Contraires
Gegensätze

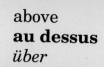

below
dessous
unter

dry
sec
trocken

wet
mouillé
naß

up
en haut
oben

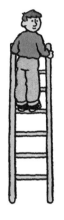

down
en bas
unten

open
ouvert
offen

closed
fermé
zu

long
long
lang

short
court
kurz

26

awake **éveillé** *wach*

asleep **endormi** *schlafend*

high **haut** *hoch*

low **bas** *niedrig*

behind **derrière** *hinter*

in front **devant** *vor*

dirty **sale** *schmutzig*

clean **propre** *sauber*

sad **triste** *traurig*

happy **heureux** *fröhlich*

back **le dos** *die Rückseite*

front **le devant** *die Vorderseite*

big **grand** *groß*

little **petit** *klein*

old **vieux** *alt*

young **jeune** *jung*

hot **chaud** *heiß*

cold **froid** *kalt*

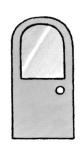

wide **large** *breit*

narrow **étroit** *schmal*

out **dehors** *draußen*

in **dans** *drinnen*

27

In the Left-Luggage Office
A la Consigne
Bei der Gepäckaufbewahrung

Ben and Polly look for their bucket and spade in the left-luggage office.

Ben et Polly cherchent leur pelle et leur seau dans la consigne.

Ben und Polly suchen ihren Eimer und ihre Schaufel bei der Gepäckaufbewahrung.

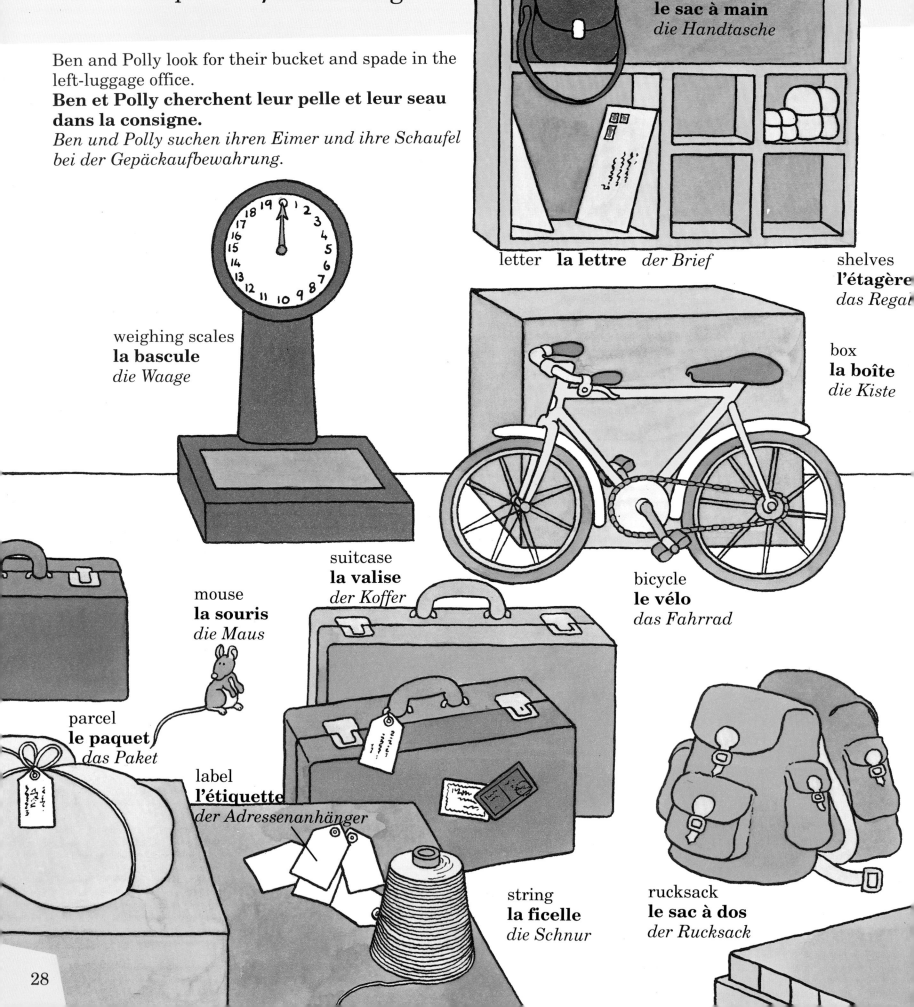

handbag
le sac à main
die Handtasche

letter **la lettre** *der Brief*

shelves
l'étagère
das Regal

box
la boîte
die Kiste

weighing scales
la bascule
die Waage

bicycle
le vélo
das Fahrrad

suitcase
la valise
der Koffer

mouse
la souris
die Maus

parcel
le paquet
das Paket

label
l'étiquette
der Adressenanhänger

string
la ficelle
die Schnur

rucksack
le sac à dos
der Rucksack

28

clock
l'horloge
die Uhr

Toby the tram engine
Toby la locomotive de tramway
Toby die Tramlokomotive

rope
la corde
das Seil

They aren't here.
Ils ne sont pas ici.
Sie sind nicht hier.

locker
le casier
das Schließfach

trunk
la malle
der Schrankkoffer

padlock
le cadenas
das Vorhängeschloß

umbrella
le parapluie
der Regenschirm

duffel bag
le sac marin
der Matchbeutel

teddy bear
le nounours
der Teddybär

crate
la caisse
die Kiste

29

The Family
La Famille
Die Familie

grandmother
la grand-mère
die Großmutter

Where are all these people going?
Où vont tous ces gens?
Wohin gehen alle diese Leute?

Gordon the big engine
Gordon la grande locomotive
Gordon die große Lokomotive

grandparents
les grands-parents
die Großeltern

grandfather
le grand-père
der Großvater

mother
la mère
die Mutter

Hello, Mummy!
Salut, Maman!
Hallo, Mutti!

Hello, Daddy!
Salut, Papa!
Hallo, Vati!

car
la voiture
das Auto

baby
le bébé
das Baby

son
le fils
der Sohn

cross
la croix
das Kreuz

tyre
le pneu
der Reifen

spire
la flèche
die Turmspitze

daughter
la fille
die Tochter

bumper
le pare-chocs
die Stoßstange

church
l'église
die Kirche

husband
le mari
der Mann

wife
la femme
die Frau

Bertie the bus
Bertie l'autobus
Bertie der Bus

Good-bye!
Au revoir!
Auf Wiedersehen!

sister
la sœur
die Schwester

brother
le frère
der Bruder

30

christening
le baptême
die Taufe

stained glass window
le vitrail
das Buntglasfenster

I name this child Thomas.
Je donne à cet enfant le nom de Thomas.
Ich taufe dieses Kind auf den Namen Thomas.

aunt
la tante
die Tante

uncle
l'oncle
der Onkel

father
le père
der Vater

parents
les parents
die Eltern

priest
le prêtre
der Pfarrer

godchild
le filleul
das Patenkind

camera
l'appareil-photo
die Kamera

font
les fonts baptismaux
der Taufstein

godmother
la marraine
die Patentante

niece
la nièce
die Nichte

grandson
le petit-fils
der Enkel

nephew
le neveu
der Neffe

godfather
le parrain
der Patenonkel

granddaughter
la petite-fille
die Enkelin

31

Numbers
Les Numéros
Die Zahlen

Can you count from one to ten?
Sais-tu compter de un à dix?
Kannst du von eins bis zehn zählen?

one
un
eins

one train
un train
ein Zug

two
deux
zwei

two fish
deux poissons
zwei Fische

three
trois
drei

three boats
trois bateaux
drei Boote

cat
le chat
die Katze

four
quatre
vier

four cats
quatre chats
vier Katzen

kitten
le chaton
das Kätzchen

five
cinq
fünf

five umbrellas
cinq parapluies
fünf Regenschirme

six
six
sechs

six friends
six amis
sechs Freunde

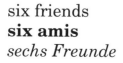

32

7

seven
sept
sieben

seven mailbags
sept sacs postaux
sieben Postsäcke

8

eight
huit
acht

eight chickens
huit poules
acht Hühner

9

nine
neuf
neun

nine passengers on the platform
neuf passagers sur le quai
neun Reisende am Bahnsteig

10

ten
dix
zehn

ten pieces of cake
dix morceaux de gâteau
zehn Stücke Kuchen

11	**12**	**13**	**14**	**15**	**16**	**17**	**18**	**19**	**20**
eleven	twelve	thirteen	fourteen	fifteen	sixteen	seventeen	eighteen	nineteen	twenty
onze	**douze**	**treize**	**quatorze**	**quinze**	**seize**	**dix-sept**	**dix-huit**	**dix-neuf**	**vingt**
elf	*zwölf*	*dreizehn*	*vierzehn*	*fünfzehn*	*sechzehn*	*siebzehn*	*achtzehn*	*neunzehn*	*zwanzig*

Professions
Les Métiers
Die Berufe

Henry the green engine
Henry la locomotive verte
Henry die grüne Lokomotive

top hat
le haut-de-forme
der Zylinder

lamp
la lampe
die Lampe

coat
le manteau
der Mantel

window
la fenêtre
das Fenster

The Fat Controller
le gros contrôleur
der dicke Direktor

office
le bureau
das Büro

pencil
le crayon
der Bleistift

ink **l'encre** *die Tinte*

sheet of paper
la feuille de papie
das Blatt Papier

chair
la chaise
der Stuhl

telephone
le téléphone
das Telefon

pen
le stylo
der Kugelschreiber

wastepaper basket
la corbeille
der Papierkorb

desk
le bureau
der Schreibtisch

The Fat Controller organises
the engines.
**Le gros contrôleur organise les
locomotives.**
*Der dicke Direktor macht einen Fahrplan
für die Lokomotiven.*

helmet
le casque
der Helm

farmer
le fermier
der Bauer

Terence the tractor
Terence le tracteur
Terence der Traktor

policeman
l'agent de police
der Polizist

What do these people do for a living?
Que font ces gens comme métier?
Was machen diese Leute beruflich?

patient
le malade
der Patient

letter
la lettre
der Brief

ladder
l'échelle
die Leiter

postman
le facteur
der Briefträger

doctor
le docteur
der Arzt

nurse
l'infirmière
die Krankenschwester

window cleaner
le laveur de vitres
der Fensterputzer

lorrydriver
le camionneur
der Lastwagenfahrer

blackboard
le tableau noir
die Tafel

teacher
le professeur
der Lehrer

lorry
le camion
der Lastwagen

water
l'eau
das Wasser

flag
le drapeau
die Flagge

fire
le feu
das Feuer

guard
le chef de train
der Schaffner

fireman
le pompier
der Feuerwehrmann

hose
le tuyau
der Feuerwehrschlauch

fire engine
la pompe à incendie
das Feuerwehrauto

35

In the Station Café
Au Café de la Gare
Im Bahnhofscafé

No one in the café has seen Ben and Polly's bucket and spade.
Personne dans le café n'a vu la pelle et le seau de Ben et Polly.
Niemand im Café hat den Eimer und die Schaufel von Ben und Polly gesehen.

window
la fenêtre
das Fenster

Thomas the tank engine
Thomas la locomotive à vapeur
Thomas die Dampflok

bird
l'oiseau
der Vogel

napkin **la serviette** *die Serviette*

fridge
le frigo
der Kühlschrank

broom
le balai
der Besen

rubbish bin
la poubelle
der Mülleimer

bucket
le seau
der Eimer

They aren't here either.
Ils ne sont pas ici non plus.
Sie sind auch nicht hier.

straw
la paille
der Trinkhalm

glass
le verre
das Glas

salt
le sel
das Salz

pepper
le poivre
der Pfeffer

orange juice
le jus d'orange
der Orangensaft

table
la table
der Tisch

tablecloth
la nappe
die Tischdecke

shelves
l'étagère
das Regal

plate
l'assiette

der Teller

cup
la tasse
die Tasse

glass
le verre
das Glas

fizzy drinks
les boissons gazeuses
die Limonaden

tea urn
la fontaine à thé
die Teemaschine

TEA

burger
le hamburger
der Hamburger

coffee pot
la cafetière
die Kaffeekanne

Crisps Crisps Crisps

counter **le comptoir** *die Theke*

banana
la banane
die Banane

biscuit
le biscuit
der Keks

crisps
les chips
die Chips

sandwich
le sandwich
die Schnitte

orange
l'orange
die Orange

apple
la pomme
der Apfel

man
l'homme
der Mann

chair
la chaise
der Stuhl

fork
la fourchette
die Gabel

spoon
la cuillère
der Löffel

saucer
la soucoupe
die Untertasse

cat
le chat
die Katze

knife
le couteau
das Messer

sugar bowl
le bol de sucre
die Zuckerdose

37

At the Zoo
Au Jardin Zoologique
Im Zoo

hippopotamus
l'hippopotame
das Nilpferd

> I like mud.
> **J'aime la boue.**
> *Der Schlamm gefällt mir.*

mud
la boue
der Schlamm

Thomas, James and Bertie are taking some animals to the zoo.
Thomas, James et Bertie transportent des animaux au zoo.
Thomas, James und Bertie bringen einige Tiere in den Zoo.

shed
le hangar
der Schuppen

> I'm fierce.
> **Je suis féroce.**
> *Ich bin wild.*

stripe
la zébrure
der Streifen

tiger
le tigre
der Tiger

> I have a very long neck.
> **J'ai le cou très long.**
> *Ich habe einen sehr langen Hals.*

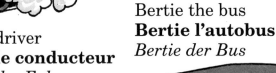

giraffe
la girafe
die Giraffe

driver
le conducteur
der Fahrer

Bertie the bus
Bertie l'autobus
Bertie der Bus

Who prefers going by bus?
Qui préfère prendre l'autobus?
Wer fährt lieber mit dem Bus?

monkey
le singe
der Affe

> I'm naughty.
> **Je suis polisson.**
> *Ich bin unartig.*

passenger
le passager
der Reisende

I'm king of the animals.
Je suis le roi des animaux.
Ich bin der König der Tiere.

I like eating bamboo.
J'aime manger le bambou.
Ich esse gern Bambus.

Which animals are already at the zoo?
Quels animaux sont déjà au zoo?
Welche Tiere sind schon im Zoo?

mane
la crinière
die Mähne

panda
le panda
der Panda

tail
la queue
der Schwanz

lion
le lion
der Löwe

bamboo
le bambou
der Bambus

crocodile
le crocodile
das Krokodil

water
l'eau
das Wasser

iceberg
l'iceberg
der Eisberg

I like snow.
J'aime la neige.
Der Schnee gefällt mir.

penguin
le pingouin
der Pinguin

tooth
la dent
der Zahn

I'm hungry.
J'ai faim.
Ich habe Hunger.

ice
la glace
das Eis

I'm huge.
Je suis énorme.
Ich bin riesig.

tree trunk
le tronc d'arbre
der Baumstamm

I like climbing.
J'aime grimper.
Ich klettere gern.

branch
la branche
der Ast

elephant
l'éléphant
der Elefant

bear
l'ours
der Bär

The Signal Box
La Cabine d'Aiguillage
Das Stellwerk

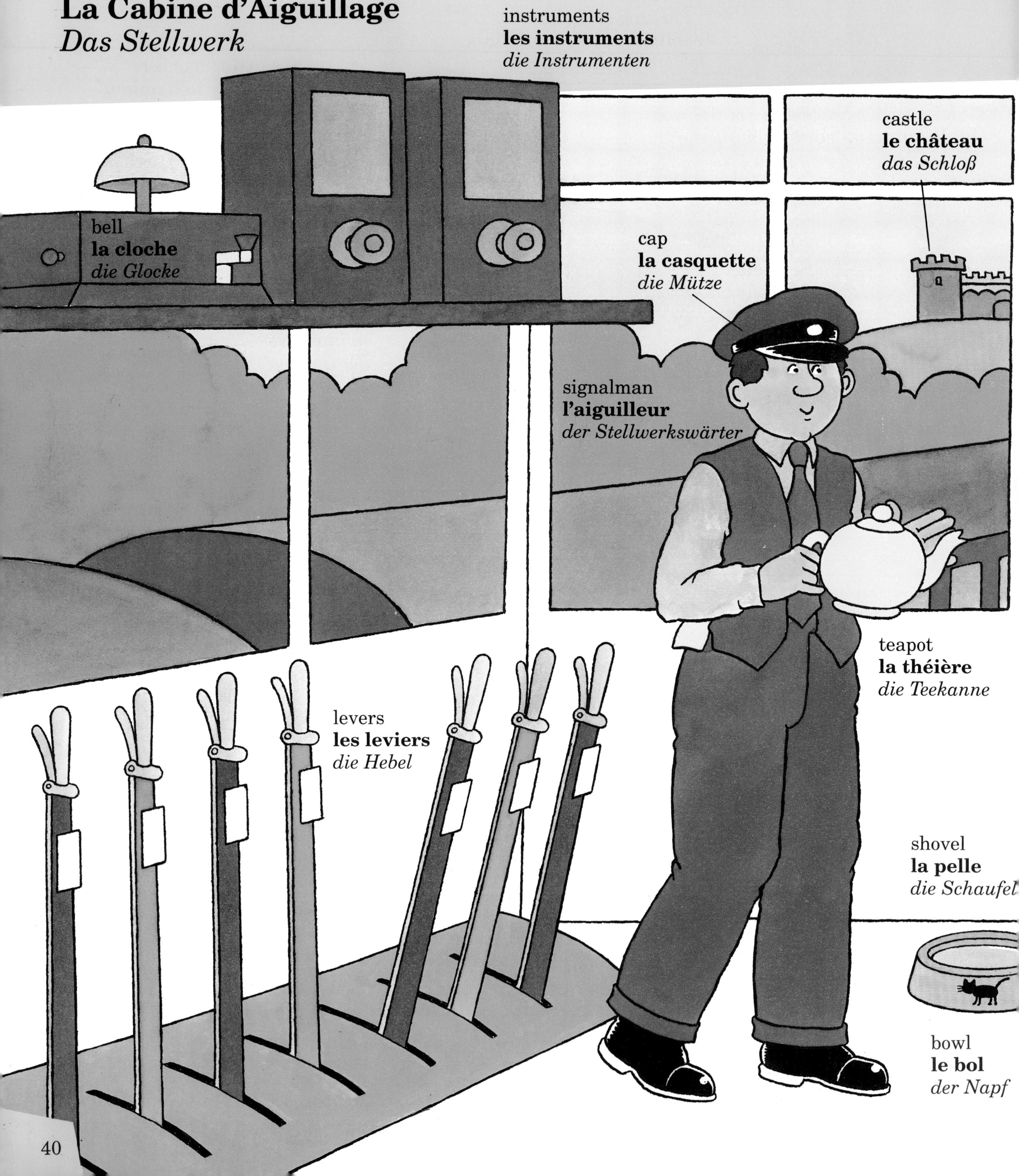

instruments
les instruments
die Instrumenten

castle
le château
das Schloß

bell
la cloche
die Glocke

cap
la casquette
die Mütze

signalman
l'aiguilleur
der Stellwerkswärter

teapot
la théière
die Teekanne

levers
les leviers
die Hebel

shovel
la pelle
die Schaufel

bowl
le bol
der Napf

40

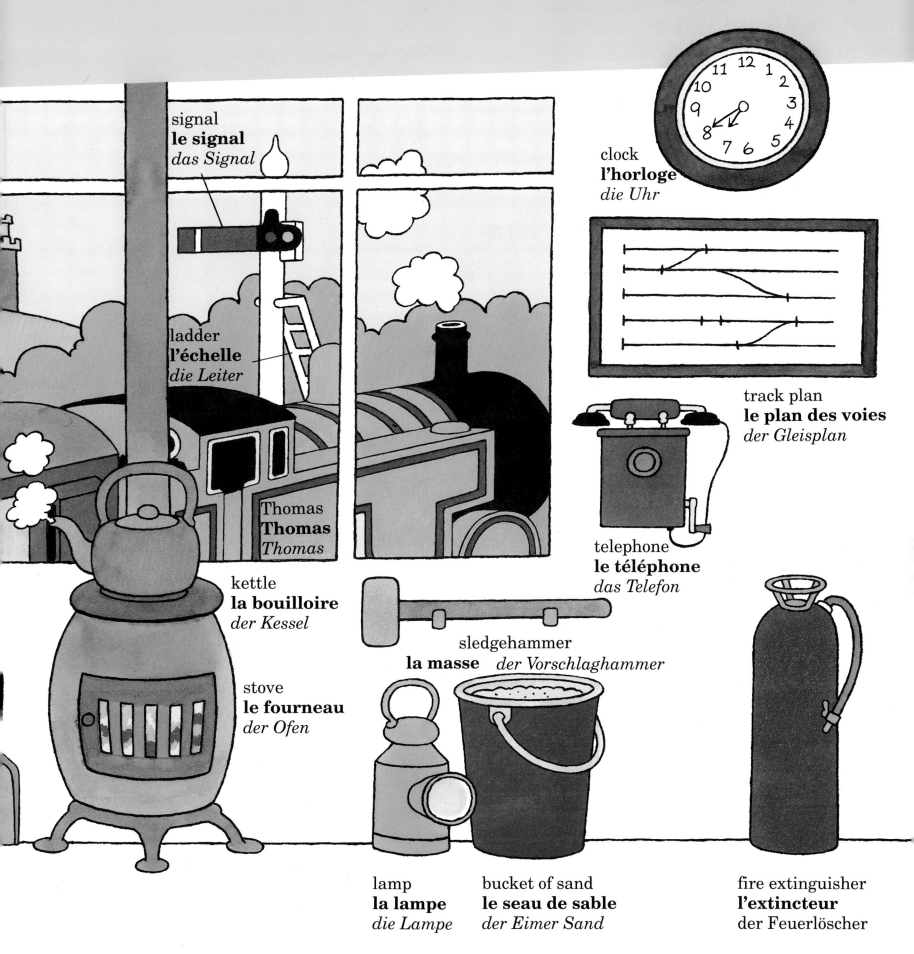

signal
le signal
das Signal

clock
l'horloge
die Uhr

ladder
l'échelle
die Leiter

track plan
le plan des voies
der Gleisplan

Thomas
Thomas
Thomas

telephone
le téléphone
das Telefon

kettle
la bouilloire
der Kessel

sledgehammer
la masse *der Vorschlaghammer*

stove
le fourneau
der Ofen

lamp
la lampe
die Lampe

bucket of sand
le seau de sable
der Eimer Sand

fire extinguisher
l'extincteur
der Feuerlöscher

The signalman is making a cup of tea.
L'aiguilleur fait une tasse de thé.
Der Stellwerkswärter macht eine Tasse Tee.

41

In the Countryside
A la Campagne
Auf dem Land

sail
l'aile
der Flügel

windmill
le moulin à vent
die Windmühle

crops
la récolte
das Getreide

roof
le toit
das Dach

chimney
la cheminée
der Schornstein

wall
le mur
die Mauer

farmhouse
la ferme
das Bauernhaus

horse
le cheval
das Pferd

bush
le buisson
der Busch

fence
la palissade
der Zaun

hoof
le sabot
der Huf

bulrush
le jonc
der Rohrkolben

water
l'eau
das Wasser

duck
le canard
die Ente

grass
l'herbe
das Gras

goose
l'oie
die Gans

rabbit
le lapin
das Kaninchen

pond
la mare
der Teich

wing
l'aile
der Flügel

beak
le bec
der Schnabel

farmyard
la basse-cour
der Hof

42

lawn
la pelouse
der Rasen

field
le champ
das Feld

cottage
la chaumière
das Häuschen

path
l'allée
der Weg

tree
l'arbre
der Baum

Thomas
Thomas
Thomas

Annie
Annie
Annie

sheep
le mouton
das Schaf

wool
la laine
die Wolle

gate
la barrière
das Gatter

cow
la vache
die Kuh

stile
l'échalier
der Zaunübertritt

fox
le renard
der Fuchs

snout
le groin
der Rüssel

pig
le cochon
das Schwein

Ben and Polly have to go home without
their bucket and spade.
**Ben et Polly doivent rentrer chez eux
sans leur pelle et leur seau.**
*Ben und Polly müssen ohne ihren Eimer
und ihre Schaufel nach Hause gehen.*

43

Travelling
Voyager
Reisen

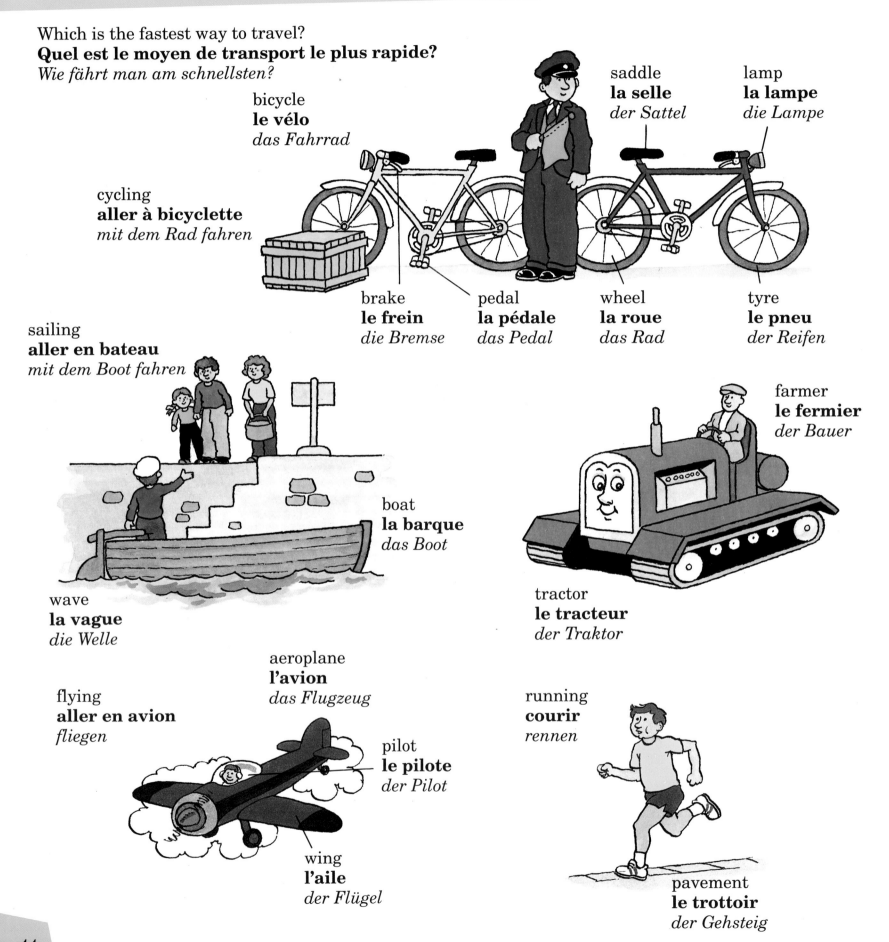

Which is the fastest way to travel?
Quel est le moyen de transport le plus rapide?
Wie fährt man am schnellsten?

bicycle
le vélo
das Fahrrad

saddle
la selle
der Sattel

lamp
la lampe
die Lampe

cycling
aller à bicyclette
mit dem Rad fahren

brake
le frein
die Bremse

pedal
la pédale
das Pedal

wheel
la roue
das Rad

tyre
le pneu
der Reifen

sailing
aller en bateau
mit dem Boot fahren

farmer
le fermier
der Bauer

boat
la barque
das Boot

wave
la vague
die Welle

tractor
le tracteur
der Traktor

aeroplane
l'avion
das Flugzeug

flying
aller en avion
fliegen

running
courir
rennen

pilot
le pilote
der Pilot

wing
l'aile
der Flügel

pavement
le trottoir
der Gehsteig

train
le train
der Zug

crash helmet
le casque
der Sturzhelm

bus
l'autobus
der Bus

motorbike
la motocyclette
das Motorrad

helicopter
l'hélicoptère
der Hubschrauber

walking
aller à pied
zu Fuß gehen

roller skate
le patin à roulettes
der Rollschuh

roller-skating
faire du patin à roulettes
Rollschuhlaufen

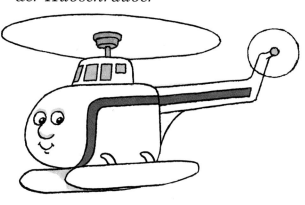

riding
aller à cheval
reiten

riding hat
la bombe
der Reithut

reins
les rênes
die Zügel

driving
aller en voiture
mit dem Auto fahren

car park
le parking
der Parkplatz

car
la voiture
das Auto

horse
le cheval
das Pferd

45

Colours
Les Couleurs
Die Farben

I'm a green engine.
Je suis une locomotive verte.
Ich bin eine grüne Lokomotive.

white **blanc** *weiß*

black **noir** *schwarz*

green **vert** *grün*

red **rouge** *rot*

orange **orange** *orange*

brown **brun** *braun*

46

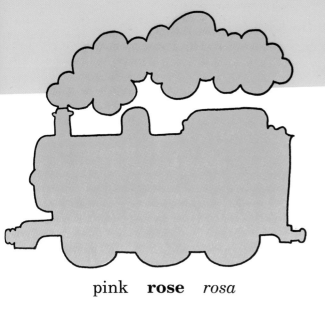

pink **rose** *rosa*

yellow **jaune** *gelb*

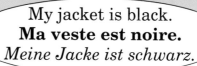

My jacket is black.
Ma veste est noire.
Meine Jacke ist schwarz.

My paws are white.
Mes pattes sont blanches.
Meine Pfoten sind weiß.

light blue **bleu clair** *hellblau*

purple **violet** *violett*

dark blue
bleu foncé
dunkelblau

blue **bleu** *blau*

grey **gris** *grau*

I have a red stripe.
J'ai une rayure rouge.
Ich habe einen roten Streifen.

47

By the River
Au Bord du Fleuve
Am Fluß

Ben and Polly are looking out of Thomas's window.
Ben et Polly regardent par la fenêtre de Thomas.
Ben und Polly sehen aus dem Fenster von Thomas.

steeple
le clocher
der Kirchturm

hill
la colline
der Hügel

bird
l'oiseau
der Vogel

tree
l'arbre
der Baum

church
l'église
die Kirche

nest
le nid
das Nest

dragonfly
la libellule
die Libelle

umbrella
le parapluie
der Regenschirm

fishing rod
la canne à pêche
die Angelrute

rock
le rocher
der Felsen

trunk
le tronc
der Stamm

bait
l'appât
der Köder

fly
la mouche
die Fliege

basket
le panier
der Korb

float
la flotte
der Schwimmer

tadpole
le têtard
die Kaulquappe

fish
le poisson
der Fisch

hook
le hameçon
der Haken

bridge
le pont
die Brücke

train
le train
der Zug

water mill
le moulin à eau
die Wassermühle

arch
l'arche
der Bogen

bush
le buisson
der Busch

wheel
la roue
das Wasserrad

river
le fleuve
der Fluß

rowing boat
la barque
das Ruderboot

oar
la rame
das Ruder

swan
le cygne
der Schwan

water rat
le rat d'eau
die Wasserratte

frog
la grenouille
der Frosch

heron
le héron
der Reiher

minnow
le vairon
die Elritze

49

Fruit and Vegetables
Les Fruits et les Légumes
Obst und Gemüse

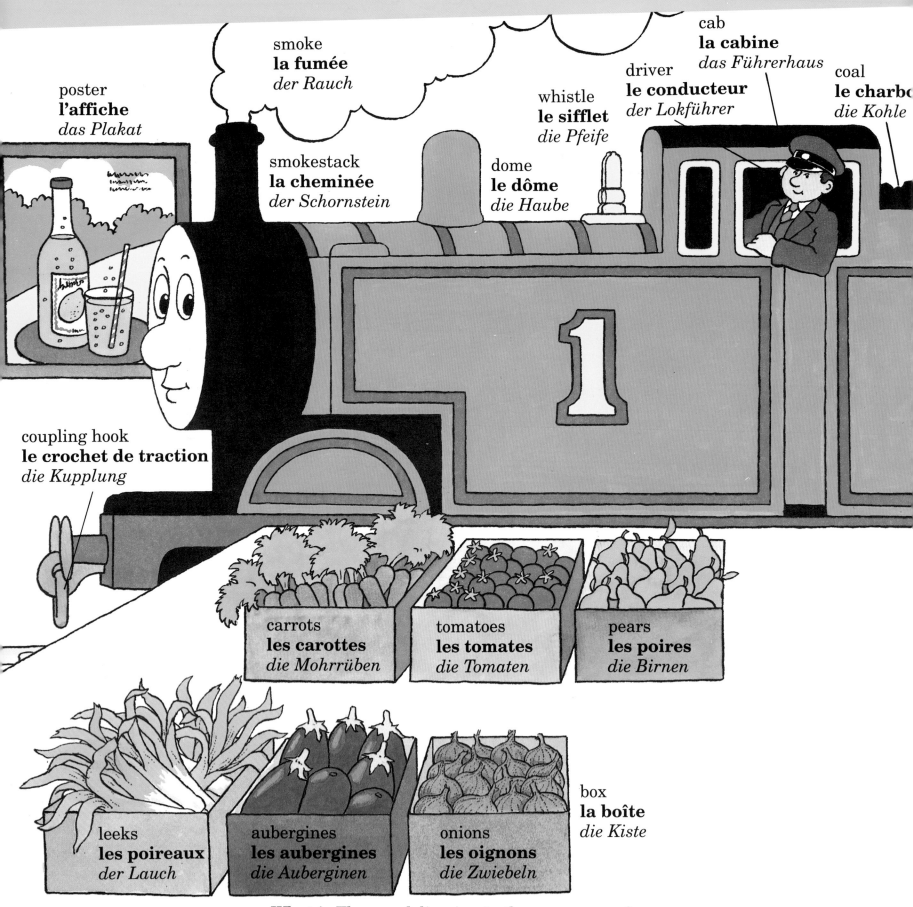

smoke
la fumée
der Rauch

cab
la cabine
das Führerhaus

poster
l'affiche
das Plakat

driver
le conducteur
der Lokführer

coal
le charbo
die Kohle

whistle
le sifflet
die Pfeife

smokestack
la cheminée
der Schornstein

dome
le dôme
die Haube

coupling hook
le crochet de traction
die Kupplung

carrots
les carottes
die Mohrrüben

tomatoes
les tomates
die Tomaten

pears
les poires
die Birnen

box
la boîte
die Kiste

leeks
les poireaux
der Lauch

aubergines
les aubergines
die Auberginen

onions
les oignons
die Zwiebeln

What is Thomas delivering to the greengrocer?
Qu'est-ce que Thomas va livrer au marchand de légumes?
Was wird Thomas am Gemüseladen abliefern?

50

greengrocer
le marchand de légumes
der Gemüsehändler

apple
la pomme
der Apfel

orange
l'orange
die Orange

banana
la banane
die Banane

pineapple
l'ananas
die Ananas

till
la caisse
die Kasse

scales
la balance
die Waage

plum
la prune
die Pflaume

peach
la pêche
der Pfirsich

cherry
la cerise
die Kirsche

grapefruit
le pamplemousse
die Pampelmuse

lemon
le citron
die Zitrone

lime
le citron vert
die Limetta

melon
le melon
die Melone

raspberry
la framboise
die Himbeere

strawberry
la fraise
die Erdbeere

apricot
l'abricot
die Aprikose

grape
le raisin
die Weintraube

potato
**la pomme
de terre**
die Kartoffel

mushroom
le champignon
der Pilz

cabbage
le chou
der Kohl

onion
l'oignon
die Zwiebel

bean
le haricot
die Bohne

garlic
l'ail
der Knoblauch

courgette
la courgette
die Zucchini

aubergine
l'aubergine
die Aubergine

cauliflower
le chou-fleur
der Blumenkohl

leek
le poireau
der Lauch

parsnip
le panais
der Pastinak

celery
le céleri
der Stangensellerie

lettuce
la laitue
der Kopfsalat

cucumber
le concombre
die Salatgurke

spinach
les épinards
der Spinat

mouse
la souris
die Maus

cat
le chat
die Katze

The Seasons of the Year
Les Saisons de l'Année
Die Jahreszeiten

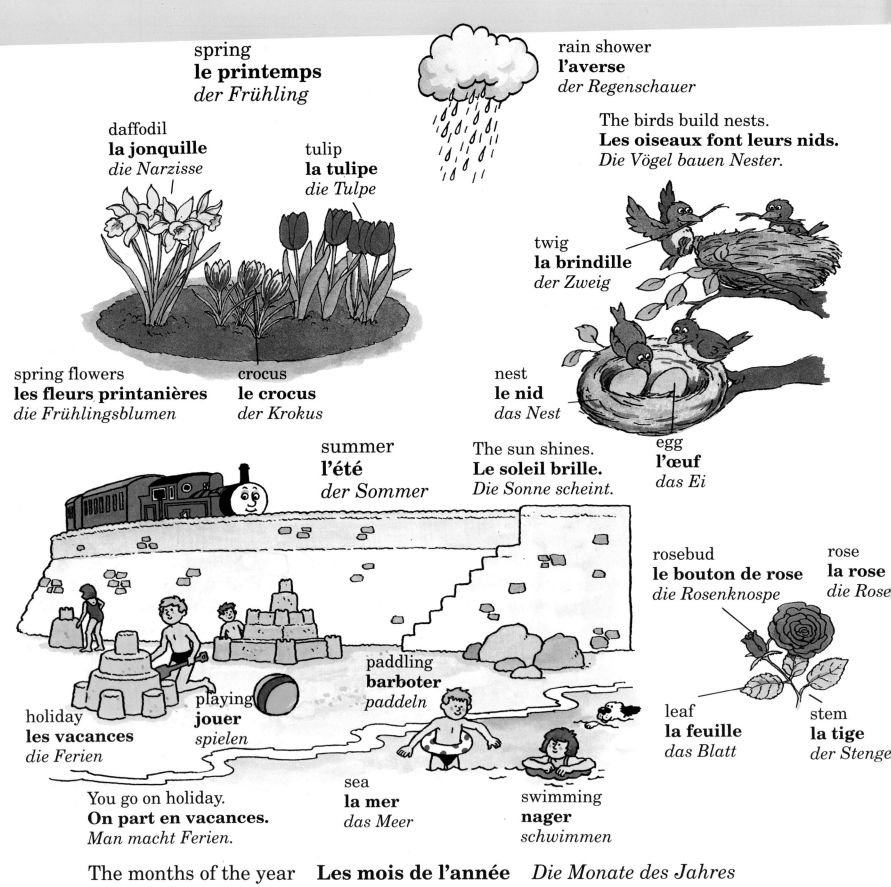

spring
le printemps
der Frühling

rain shower
l'averse
der Regenschauer

daffodil
la jonquille
die Narzisse

tulip
la tulipe
die Tulpe

The birds build nests.
Les oiseaux font leurs nids.
Die Vögel bauen Nester.

twig
la brindille
der Zweig

spring flowers
les fleurs printanières
die Frühlingsblumen

crocus
le crocus
der Krokus

nest
le nid
das Nest

summer
l'été
der Sommer

The sun shines.
Le soleil brille.
Die Sonne scheint.

egg
l'œuf
das Ei

rosebud
le bouton de rose
die Rosenknospe

rose
la rose
die Rose

paddling
barboter
paddeln

playing
jouer
spielen

holiday
les vacances
die Ferien

leaf
la feuille
das Blatt

stem
la tige
der Stenge

You go on holiday.
On part en vacances.
Man macht Ferien.

sea
la mer
das Meer

swimming
nager
schwimmen

The months of the year   **Les mois de l'année**   *Die Monate des Jahres*

January	February	March	April	May	June
janvier	**février**	**mars**	**avril**	**mai**	**juin**
Januar	*Februar*	*März*	*April*	*Mai*	*Juni*

autumn
l'automne
der Herbst

blackberry
la mûre
die Brombeere

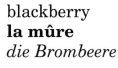

apple tree
le pommier
der Apfelbaum

thorn
l'épine
der Dorn

The leaves fall.
Les feuilles tombent.
Die Blätter fallen.

satchel
le cartable
die Schultasche

back to school
la rentrée des classes
die Schulen fangen wieder an

harvest
la récolte
die Ernte

winter
l'hiver
der Winter

snowflake
le flocon de neige
die Schneeflocke

fir tree
le sapin
der Tannenbaum

snow
la neige
der Schnee

snowball
la boule de neige
der Schneeball

robin
le rouge-gorge
das Rotkehlchen

holly
le houx
die Stechpalme

toboggan
la luge
der Schlitten

ivy
le lierre
der Efeu

snowman
le bonhomme de neige
der Schneemann

July	August	September	October	November	December
juillet	**août**	**septembre**	**octobre**	**novembre**	**décembre**
Juli	*August*	*September*	*Oktober*	*November*	*Dezember*

At the Station
A la Gare
Am Bahnhof

Ben and Polly have found their bucket and spade.
Ben et Polly ont trouvé leur pelle et leur seau.
Ben und Polly haben ihren Eimer und ihre Schaufel gefunden.

streetlamp
le réverbère
die Straßenlaterne

roof
le toit
das Dach

tree
l'arbre
der Baum

vending machine
la machine de vente
der Verkäuferautomat

TIDMOUTH

station
la gare
der Bahnhof

Percy
Percy
Percy

guard
le chef de train
der Schaffner

spade
la pelle
die Schaufel

newspaper
le journal
die Zeitung

cat
le chat
die Katze

flower
la fleur
die Blume

bucket
le seau
der Eimer

54

What else do they see at the station?
Qu'est-ce qu'ils voient d'autre à la gare?
Was sehen sie sonst noch am Bahnhof?

flag
le drapeau
die Flagge

ticket collector
le contrôleur
der Schaffner

ticket
le billet
die Fahrkarte

whistle
le sifflet
die Pfeife

Tickets, please!
Vos billets, s'il vous plaît!
Ihre Fahrkarten, bitte!

suitcase
la valise
der Koffer

passenger
le passager
der Reisende

guard
le chef de train
der Schaffner

timetable
l'horaire
der Fahrplan

VICARSTOWN	ARLESBURGH
6·00 · 6·30	7·10 · 7·40
7·00 · 7·30	8·40
8·00 · 8·30	9·40
9·00 · 9·30	0·40
10·00 · 10·30	11·40
11·00 · 11·30	12·40

driver
le conducteur
der Lokführer

fireman
le chauffeur
der Heizer

engine
la locomotive
die Lokomotive

Fat Controller
le gros contrôleur
der dicke Direktor

rails
les rails
die Schienen

buffers
les tampons
der Prellbock

Going Shopping
Faire des Courses
Einkaufen

On the way home, Ben and Polly go shopping with their mother.
Sur le chemin du retour, Ben et Polly font des courses avec leur mère.
Auf dem Heimweg gehen Ben und Polly mit ihrer Mutter einkaufen.

They catch the bus outside the station.
Ils prennent l'autobus devant la gare.
Sie nehmen den Bus vor dem Bahnhof.

bus stop
l'arrêt d'autobus
die Bushaltestelle

Bertie the bus
Bertie l'autobus
Bertie der Bus

supermarket
le supermarché
der Supermarkt

shopping list
la liste des achats
der Einkaufszettel

shelves
le rayon
das Regal

shopping trolley
le chariot
der Einkaufswagen

aisle
l'allée
der Gang

shopping basket
le panier
der Einkaufskorb

customer
le client
der Kunde

56

What do they buy?
Qu'est-ce qu'ils achètent?
Was kaufen sie?

tissues
les mouchoirs en papier
die Papiertaschentücher

flour
la farine
das Mehl

sugar
le sucre
der Zucker

butter
le beurre
die Butter

cream
la crème
die Sahne

yogurt
le yaourt
der Joghurt

milk
le lait
die Milch

cheese
le fromage
der Käse

eggs
les œufs
die Eier

biscuits
les biscuits
die Kekse

sweets
les bonbons
die Bonbons

cake
le gâteau
der Kuchen

chocolate
le chocolat
die Schokolade

oil
l'huile
das Öl

vinegar
le vinaigre
der Essig

salt
le sel
das Salz

pepper
le poivre
der Pfeffer

herbs
les fines herbes
die Kräuter

jam
la confiture
die Marmelade

honey
le miel
der Honig

peanut butter
le beurre de cacahouètes
die Erdnußbutter

orange juice
le jus d'orange
der Orangensaft

ice cream
la glace
das Eis

ham **le jambon**
der Schinken

bacon
le lard
der Speck

meat
la viande
das Fleisch

fish
le poisson
der Fisch

toilet paper
le papier hygiénique
das Toilettenpapier

shampoo
le shampooing
das Haarwaschmittel

soap
le savon
die Seife

carrier bag
le sac en plastique
die Tragetüte

cotton wool
l'ouate
die Watte

toothpaste
le dentifrice
die Zahncreme

washing powder
la lessive
das Waschpulver

fizzy drinks
les boissons gazeuses
die Limonaden

What Time is it?
Quelle Heure est-il?
Wieviel Uhr ist es?

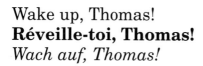

Wake up, Thomas!
Réveille-toi, Thomas!
Wach auf, Thomas!

breakfast.
le petit déjeuner.
das Frühstück

tea
le thé
der Tee

plate
l'assiette
der Teller

mug
la tasse
der Becher

alarm clock
le réveil
der Wecker

fried egg
l'œuf au plat
das Spiegelei

bacon
le lard
der Speck

toast
le pain gri
der Toast

It's quarter past seven.
Il est sept heures et quart.
Es ist Viertel nach sieben.

It's nine o'clock
Il est neuf heures.
Es ist neun Uhr.

Thomas goes to work.
Thomas va au travail.
Thomas geht arbeiten.

one o'clock
une heure
ein Uhr

two o'clock
deux heures
zwei Uhr

three o'clock
trois heures
drei Uhr

four o'clock
quatre heures
vier Uhr

five o'clock
cinq heures
fünf Uhr

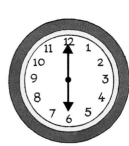

six o'clock
six heures
sechs Uhr

It's quarter to six.
Il est six heures moins le quart.
Es ist Viertel vor sechs.

The engines go home.
Les locomotives rentrent à la maison.
Die Lokomotiven gehen nach Hause.

It's half past eight.
Il est huit heures et demie.
Es ist halb neun.

Thomas goes to bed.
Thomas se couche.
Thomas geht zu Bett.

Good night, Thomas!
Bonne nuit, Thomas!
Gute Nacht, Thomas!

Sleep well
Dors bien.
Schlaf gut.

sun
le soleil
die Sonne

moon
la lune
der Mond

owl
le hibou
die Eule

midday
midi
Mittag

midnight
minuit
Mitternacht

seven o'clock
sept heures
sieben Uhr

eight o'clock
huit heures
acht Uhr

nine o'clock
neuf heures
neun Uhr

ten o'clock
dix heures
zehn Uhr

eleven o'clock
onze heures
elf Uhr

twelve o'clock
douze heures
zwölf Uhr

How to say French words

Some letters sound the same in French and German as they do in English, but others are quite different. The following guidelines may help you:

a   usually sounds like the **a** in h**a**t
matin, tasse,

au, eau   sound like the **oa** in t**oa**st
automne, eau,

c   before "e" or "i" sounds like the **s** in **s**un
cette, ici

c   before any other letter sounds like the **c** in **c**at
campagne, école

ç   sounds like the **s** in **s**un
français, glaçage

ch   sounds like the **sh** in **sh**ip
chemise, chapeau, brioche

e, eu   sound like the **a** in **a**bove
le, chemise, feu

é, er, ez   sound like the **ay** in d**ay**
métier, jouer, nez

è, ê   sound like the **e** in r**e**d
mère, fenêtre

g   before "e" or "i" sounds like the **s** in mea**s**ure
gelée, girafe

g   before any other letter sounds like the **g** in **g**o
goûter, gâteau, gris

gn   sounds like the **n** in **n**ew
campagne, poignet

h   is usually silent
herbe, huit

i, y   sound like the **i** in mach**i**ne
cuisine, dîner, pyjama

j   sounds like the **s** in mea**s**ure
jardin, jeu

ll   after an "i", sounds like the **y** in **y**oung
famille, oreiller

o   usually sounds like the **o** in h**o**t
fromage, bol

œu   sounds like the **u** in f**u**r
sœur, cœur

oi   sounds like the "wa" sound in **one**
mois, pois

ou   sounds like the **oo** in z**oo**
cou, soucoupe

qu   sounds like the **k** in **k**ite
qui, queue

r   is rolled or trilled at the back of the throat

th   sounds like the **t** in **t**op
thé, bibliothèque

u   sounds like the **u** in c**u**te
numéro, fumée

ui, uy   sound like the **wee** in **wee**k
cuisine, nuit, tuyau

w   sounds like the **v** in **v**ase
wagon

In French most consonants which fall at the end of a word are silent, e.g. cana**rd**, moi**s**, peti**t**, anima**ux**, pon**t**, cor**ps**, spor**t**, blan**c**, dra**p**, li**t**, bra**s**, doi**gt**.

How to say German words

ä   sounds like the **a** in c**a**re
Mädchen, Bär

au   sounds like the **ow** in n**ow**
kaufen, Maus

äu   sounds like the **oy** in b**oy**
Fräulein

ch   sounds like the **ch** in the Scottish word 'lo**ch**'
Koch

d   sounds like the **d** in **d**oor except when it is at the end of a word. Then it sounds like the **t** in **t**able
Rad, Wand

e   at the end of a word it sounds like the **a** in **a**bove.
Katze

ee   sounds like the **ay** in s**ay**
See

ei   sounds like the **i** in l**i**ne
Ei, frei, klein

eu   sounds like the **oy** in b**oy**
teuer, Feuer

g   sounds like the **g** in **g**arden
gut, Garten

i   sounds like the **i** in beg**i**n
Freundin

ie   sounds like the **ee** in r**ee**d
Lied

j   sounds like the **y** in **y**oung
jeder, Junge

o   usually sounds like the **o** in **o**pen
ober

ö   sounds like the **u** in f**u**r
öffnen

qu   sounds like **kv**
bequem

s   sounds like the **sh** in **sh**ip when followed by any other letter
Sturm, Spiegel

s   sounds like the **s** in **s**un when followed by any other letter
Sturm, Spiegel

sch   sounds like the **sh** in **sh**ip
Tisch

ß   is often written instead of **ss**. It sounds like the **s** in bu**s**.
Fuß

th   sounds like the **t** in **t**able
Thomas

u   sounds like the **oo** in r**oo**t
gut

ü   sounds like the **u** in c**u**te
über, Tür

v   sounds like the **f** in **f**ish
vier, Vogel

w   sounds like the **v** in **v**ase
Wasser

z   sounds like **ts**
Zimmer

In German, every letter in a word is pronounced, so make sure you say the **g**, **k** and **p** at the beginning of words like **g**nädige, **K**nöpfe and **P**flanze.
Don't forget to pronounce the **e** at the end of them, too.